DOGGY DOS AND DON'TS

R. J. Fischer

Pinnacle Books
http://www.pinnaclebooks.com

PINNACLE BOOKS are published by

Kensington Publishing Corp.
850 Third Avenue
New York, NY 10022

Pinnacle and the P logo Reg. U.S. Pat. & TM Off.

First Printing: October, 1997
10 9 8 7 6 5 4 3 2 1

Printed in the United States of America

This book is dedicated to Melanie & Kurt,
who know it's all true—and then some!

And thanks to Sue & Dr. Hagaman for
taking care
of all our furry friends.

It's instinctive to shake when you're wet. Make sure you do it in front of a person.

Make friends with the children. They'll sneak you food from their plates.

If they try to make you sleep outside, howl all night until they decide your place is in the house.

1

Convince them to buy you a doggy door by demanding to go out at least thirty times a day.

There is no dog run that a smart puppy can't get out of.

Learn to bark when someone approaches the door. They'll think you're guarding them and you'll get a treat.

Let all telephone callers hear you bark
at least once.

If you lay down in front of the
children's door and look very sad,
they'll let you in to sleep on their beds.

If Mommy gives you a bath and towels
you off, there's still enough water left
to splatter the mirror when you shake.

Don't fall for the old "distract the dog while I give him his medicine" trick.

Learn to bring in the newspaper. You can get in a couple of good chews that way.

If they buy you a fancy dog bed, refuse to go near it.

There's no reason to eat dog food when people food is available.

Practice making "sad puppy eyes" in front of the mirror. It'll get you almost anything you want.

Even if you'd rather sleep, jump up and greet them joyously when they come home. They need lots of love.

Sneeze a lot after Daddy gives you a bath with the hose. He'll take you into the nice warm bathtub next time.

5

If you pretend to watch television, everyone will think it's cute.

Be sneaky. Never let anyone know that you can reach the top of the table.

Laps are nice. Crawl into them at every opportunity.

If you're hungry, sit under the baby's highchair. Something will be sure to drop on the floor.

Only chase the cat when Mommy and Daddy aren't home.

If you have an "accident" in the house, act contrite and whimper a lot. They'll forgive you.

Always remember to hide the evidence. If you forget and chew a rug, drag it out and bury it behind the garage.

People beds are always more comfortable than doggy beds.

Learn the difference between shoes and food. They'll be so grateful, they'll buy you a whole box of rawhide.

If you pretend you're afraid to go to the vet, they'll pet you the entire time you're there.

Never let them know that you figured out how to open the refrigerator.

Chasing your tail is a silly thing to do, but it'll always earn you a treat.

Eat the cat's food but never let them catch you doing it.

Mommy and Daddy hate bills. Do them a real favor and chew up the envelopes before they see them.

Regard all professional dog-walkers as enemies.

9

The teacher thinks saying that the dog ate your homework is just an excuse. Prove she's wrong.

Lay your head in Daddy's lap and look at him with pure adoration. That's good for at least two treats.

If you don't like the brush they use, hide it.

Chase ice cubes when they fall on the floor. For some reason, people think that's cute.

There's always plenty of cold water in the toilet bowl.

Cats are funny to watch when they're stuck at the top of a tree.

It's fun to get the cat in trouble. They'll never guess you're the one who took everything out of the litter box.

The groomer may try to brush your teeth. This is a barbaric custom that should be resisted at all costs.

The vet is lying. Shots hurt.

Humans want to please you, but they must be well trained.

Daddy may try to train you to hunt. At the first sound of a gun, cower and hide under the car.

Be ferocious with burglars unless they bring you a big steak.

Practice knocking fragile objects off low places with your tail.

Cats were put on this earth for a purpose, but no one knows what it is.

Sweep everything off the coffee table at least once a day.

Regard all baby-sitters as enemies.

Show the burglars that your bite is much worse than your bark.

A dirty dog is a happy dog.

Don't believe them when they tell you that table food isn't good for you.

If someone's afraid of you, climb all over them.

When in doubt, shed.

Always be the first one out the door, even if it means tripping someone.

Convince Mommy that you're good protection by barking ferociously when a salesman comes to the door.

Mommy is the one who takes care of you. Be sure to let her know that you love Daddy best.

Practice looking heartbroken if they don't take you with them.

You can dig under almost anything.

Drool whenever possible.

You can chew through a table leg if you keep at it.

15

Refuse to do anything unless you get a treat.

Don't be fooled. "Bad dog" never applies to you.

Cats are for chasing.

Squirrels are for barking.

People are for licking.

If you're big, learn to slobber. If you're small, learn to yip.

When they come home from a restaurant, the little white bag is for you.

Remember the lessons of puppyhood. You know what a newspaper on the floor is for.

If they take you to obedience school, refuse to do your homework.

Pretend to be a slow learner. You'll have to do less that way.

Your primary directive: Be cute.

They may give you a silly haircut. Put up with the indignity stoically.

When Daddy barbecues, be on your best behavior. Good things are coming.

If they let you out in the middle of the night, be sure to take plenty of time to find just the right spot.

The staircase was built just for you. Race up and down at least ten times a day to get your exercise.

Remember . . . the kitty-litter tray is fair game.

If the groomer puts ribbons behind your ears, make sure you eat them before they come to pick you up.

Whenever you crave attention, whimper.

Humans need to know tricks. Teach yours to throw a ball.

Once you have found a piece of rawhide, never let it go.

There is no such thing as a nice kitty.

If you're bored, bark at something.

When Daddy eats ice cream, gently rest your head on his knee and look up at him soulfully.

Always come when called . . . unless there's something more interesting.

Practice slipping your collar.

Leave pieces of wet, slimy rawhide where Mommy and Daddy can step on them.

Always be polite to visiting dogs. Walk right up and smell their bottoms.

If you run through the mud before you come inside, you can decorate the floor with your footprints.

If Mommy plants anything, dig it up. If it still grows, eat it.

A wet tongue hath power to soothe away wrath.

Always try to sleep in front of the fireplace. They'll think it's picturesque.

Mommy and Daddy just love to have you in bed with them . . . especially between them.

Bark at falling leaves.

Bark at passing birds.

Bark at all possible occasions. They love the sound of your voice.

They'll think it's cute if you learn to snore.

Never forget . . . your mission in life is to lay around and look beautiful.

Hide one of Dad's slippers. When he asks where it is, find it. He'll think you're very smart.

Never let them know you understand every word they say. You've got to have an edge.

24

If Mommy doesn't let you have a bone, be patient. You can always dig it out of the trash later.

Sofas are delicious.

Show them that your doggy bed has cedar chips inside.

If your food bowl's empty, shove it around with your nose. They'll think it's clever and feed you.

People love to teach you tricks. It's degrading, but it keeps them happy.

Learn to howl.

People love it when you jump up on them, especially if they're all dressed up.

Playing with your squeaky toy is more fun in the middle of the night.

Never play outside when you can play inside.

Mommy and Daddy's bed is a good place to store your bones.

Be a picky eater, and you'll get to try lots of new dog food.

There's always mud somewhere in the park.

27

Never sleep on the floor if there's an available lap.

Ladies will get freaked if you poke your cold nose under their skirts.

Don't be fooled. Medicine is *not* a treat.

28

Crawl under the bed. Mommy will look
funny down on her hands and knees,
trying to coax you out.

"No" means "maybe," unless it's
shouted.

Dining is a social occasion. Bring a few
pieces of kibble into the living room and
eat them on the rug.

Categorically refuse to learn the meaning of the word "heel."

There's no reason to walk if you can run.

You'll be able to get there faster if you climb into the front seat of the car.

Lick the children's faces. There may be food on them.

Identify every hiding place in the house.

Don't come unless they call you nicely.

If they name you something silly like "Bingo" or "Spot," refuse to learn it until they come up with something more dignified.

Be very sneaky, and it'll take them months to realize that you can reach the top of the kitchen counter.

Let all the other dogs know that it's your car by putting lots of your nose-prints on the windows.

Blame the cat.

Teach Mommy to cook an extra piece, just for you.

Contrary to what they may tell you, begging is not undignified.

You can get rid of the cat for hours if you chase her up a tree.

A cold nose is a fine introduction.

Barbecues are hot. Wait until Daddy takes the meat off the grill before you snag a piece.

If a human holds you, you can be taller than all the other dogs.

Make them roll down the windows in the car so you can stick out your head.

When the car keys come out, make sure you look hopeful.

34

Humans can be careless. Never nap under the car.

Balls are for throwing.

Socks are for tugging.

Hands are for petting.

Toys are for chewing up into microscopic-sized pieces.

Pretend you're afraid of the vacuum
cleaner and attack it.

If they put all your toys in a basket,
take them back out and put them where
they belong.

Remember, their sole purpose in life is
to play with you.

It may be very difficult, but pretend you like the cat.

Learn the art of the snarl.

When Mommy and Daddy are hugging, barge in between them. You need a little affection, too.

37

Eat lots of grass. You'll be able to throw up giant green balls.

If you bark every time someone comes to the door, they won't have to buy a doorbell.

Make sure your yard is free of birds, squirrels, rodents, and marauding cats.

If they buy you a fancy doghouse, refuse to go inside.

You can keep track of every place you've been if you keep your paws nice and muddy.

If you're a small dog and you bark very loudly, everyone will think you're much bigger.

39

Start wagging your tail the moment they take out the leash.

There's no limit to what humans will give you if you look cute enough.

Learn to open doors by yourself. They'll think it's a great trick . . . at first.

Teach them the wisdom of shaking out their shoes before they put them on.

If the kids try to dress you up in their clothes, endure it. There'll be a treat when they're through.

Whining will get you lots of nice things if you use it sparingly.

Make sure at least part of your body is in every picture they take.

Learn to poke the doggy door with your paw to make certain it's open.

If you hide your kibble under the couch cushions, you'll always have extra food in a pinch.

42

Don't let them know that you can open the cupboard where they keep the backup package of treats.

If they buy you a silly collar, bury it somewhere in the yard.

A good place to hide is the fancy doghouse you've refused to use. They'll never think to look for you there.

43

Terrorize the baby-sitter. She'll give you a bone just to keep you pacified.

It's impossible to make a collar that a smart dog can't slip.

Baby toys are much more interesting than the silly things they make for dogs.

If you get under Mommy's feet when she clears the dinner table, some of the leftovers may fall on the floor.

There are lots of interesting things in the trash. Teach them the wisdom of buying covered wastebaskets.

Eat anything that even remotely resembles food.

It's in your best interest to be nice to the mailman, especially if he carries a can of pepper spray.

Even a small dog can pull someone over if he gets a running start on a leash.

Teach them not to set out appetizers on the coffee table.

Never chase cars unless you enjoy getting a snootful of exhaust fumes.

Practice looking mournful when they leave without you. They'll give you a treat to keep you happy while they're gone.

Never piddle in the same place twice. Those little yellow spots on the lawn give it color.

Bark at the garbage truck when it takes away all that wonderful stuff.

Prove that the spray they make to keep doggies off the furniture doesn't work.

Bark at your reflection in the mirror. You know it's not another dog, but they'll think it's cute.

Pick out the one person in the room who doesn't like dogs and zero right in on him or her.

48

The can opener is your friend. Come running every time anyone uses it.

Learn which way the refrigerator door opens, and make sure you're always in a perfect position to stick your head inside.

Learn to catch treats in midair. You'll get more that way.

Plop down on people's feet whenever you can.

If someone gets up in the middle of the night, follow them. They could be going to make a sandwich.

You can get away with almost anything if you crawl on your belly and whimper when they discover what you've done.

If the food they've dropped is too hot to eat, stand over it and guard it until it cools.

Warning: Electrical wires bite if they're chewed.

Bones from chicken or fish aren't good for puppies. Teach them that they should carry them out to the trash right away.

Stuffed toys can have interesting things inside.

Teach Daddy that he shouldn't buy leather briefcases.

Fresh air is good for humans. Make them take you out often.

If they're foolish enough to have white carpeting, make sure you convince them to replace it with a darker color.

The couch is yours. Sprawl out so no one else can sit on it.

If you chew on the remote control, you can change the channel.

If anyone starts to roll up a newspaper, run and hide.

Learn all the tricks they teach you, but only perform for treats.

Remind them to clean the swimming pool filter by going for a swim several times a day.

If they bring a new puppy into the house, make sure you teach it who's boss.

Your tail can be tucked up under your belly so the baby can't grab it.

Nothing looks more pathetic than a wet puppy. If you play your cards right, you can make them towel you off.

Fertilizer is good for the lawn, and it smells great. Open that big bag they bought and roll it in.

Establish guidelines early. One trick
equals several treats.

If they try to coax you into the shower,
run and hide.

Skunks smell bad. The only thing worse
is the tomato juice they'll pour all over
you to neutralize the smell.

If they try to put reindeer antlers on
you at Christmas, shake them off.

Many presents under the Christmas tree are edible.

Thanksgiving means turkey. Make sure you get your share from every person at the table.

They may try to feed you the core from an apple or the unpopped kernels from a bowl of popcorn. Hold out for something more palatable.

When the baby toddles around with a sandwich, it's food on the hoof.

If you crawl up on a chair, you can reach the top of the dining room table.

Bark loudly to scare Mommy when she takes a pan of cookies out of the oven. She may drop one.

57

Encourage your puppy friends to dig in under the fence. Your humans have company. Why shouldn't you?

Sleep when they're not home so you can be wide-eyed and alert all night.

If you bark to let them know you're there, they won't stumble over you in the middle of the night.

Teach them that giving you something tasty to put in your mouth will make you stop barking.

Always check the sliding glass door to make sure it's open before you race out to chase that thing in the yard.

"Spaying" and "neutering" are human words for something extremely unpleasant.

Whine all the way to the boarding kennel. If you make them feel guilty enough, they may decide to take you along on their next vacation.

Never let them know that you can jump the fence.

Make sure you mark every spot in the yard so the other dogs will know where you live.

Greet Mommy with a big kiss when she comes home from the grocery store. There's probably something for you.

Never let them leave you at the vet's overnight.

Learn to sit up on your hind legs and look hungry. Someone may give you a treat.

Never chew the sports page before Daddy's read it.

Refuse to eat when you're being boarded. When they come to pick you up, they'll feel guilty and give you all sorts of treats.

Cuddle up next to them when it's cold outside, and they'll let you sleep in their bed.

If you chew through those little Styrofoam boxes in the trash, you may find part of a hamburger.

A cat is not a suitable companion for a dog.

Practice looking like you're starving so the guests will feed you under the table.

63

If you sleep with one ear open, you'll hear the refrigerator door from anywhere in the house.

Dogs are a lot smarter than cats, but cats have sharper claws.

Porcupines are not fun to play with.

Make friends with neighbors who don't have dogs, especially if they eat lots of meat with bones.

Stay alert around things with wheels.

If you have light-colored fur, shed on dark-colored things.

If you have dark-colored fur, shed on light-colored things.

If you chew the sofa when they're gone, claw it a little around the edges of the hole. They may think the cat did it.

65

It's counterproductive to beg from a vegetarian.

Learn to fetch. They'll think it's cute and give you a treat.

If you get careless and fall off the bed, pretend that you meant to do it all along.

Never give up your ball without a good game of tug.

Snow is fun. Make sure you bring lots of it inside to play with later.

If Mommy gives the baby two cookies, one is rightfully yours.

Get them up early on Saturday and Sunday. Why should they sleep when they can play with you?

67

If the kids watch cartoons in the morning, they may not notice if you eat their cereal.

A declawed cat is much more fun.

Buffet dinners are great. There's always someone who'll be foolish enough to leave their plate at doggy height.

Give Mommy lots of kisses if she buys bone-in roasts.

68

Teach the cat to have a healthy respect for you, but do it when Mommy and Daddy aren't home.

They may bring a real tree inside for Christmas. Don't make the mistake of peeing on it.

Learn how to jump up and turn on the light switch. They'll think it's cute . . . at first.

69

If you want to see kitty do acrobatics, chase her onto a freshly waxed floor. (Remember to stop at the doorway.)

Get into the catnip and watch kitty try to figure out why she suddenly likes you.

Many words mean food. Increase your vocabulary by learning them all.

A rose garden is not a good place to lift your leg, especially if you're just learning.

Pretend not to understand when they ask you to do something silly, like staying in the other room when there's food on the table.

The three keys to being housebroken are: anticipation, notification, and elimination.

Toddlers put everything in their mouths. Make sure your tail is always out of reach.

If you see a truck with cages in the back, run home as fast as you can.

Never, ever confuse a person's leg with a fire hydrant.

Drink lots of water so you have to go out more often. You'll get a treat each time you do.

Never admit that you're no longer a puppy.

73

Misbehave at the groomer's. If you're lucky, they'll refuse to groom you again.

Never play with an expensive doggy toy more than once.

It may look like a ball, but if they hang it on the Christmas tree, it's not.

If you pant loudly enough, they'll turn on the air-conditioning.

When you see the can of flea spray, run and hide.

Deworming is every bit as bad as it sounds.

Grandmas are always good for just one more treat.

Prove that the dog trainer obviously never had a puppy of his own.

Show them that shedding season lasts
all year long.

Put up a gallant fight if they try to dip
you for fleas. They may give up and get
the expensive flea pills from the vet.

If you're doing something cute and they
get the camera, stop before they can
take the picture. When they put the
camera away, do something cute again.

If they leave the breakable items where you can reach them, teach them to be more careful.

The word "no" doesn't mean anything. People just like to say it.

Clamp your mouth shut when they try to give you a pill, but eat it right away if they hide it in a hotdog or a piece of cheese.

Crawl into tight places where they can't reach you.

Eat the crayons. They're nontoxic, but everyone'll freak out.

Learn to grab the end of the toilet paper and pull it all off the roll.

If you don't like something, growl. If you do like something, wag your tail. It may take a while, but they'll catch on.

Pretend you're stuck in the crawl space under the house.

When they ask you what you're doing, always look innocent.

Warning: If they say something is good for you, you're not going to like it.

Listen for the phrase, "Be a good boy," or "Be a good girl." It usually precedes something very unpleasant.

Don't be fooled. The food in your doggy
bowl is never as good as the food on
their plates.

Some flowers are edible. Make them
find out which ones they are.

Treasure hunts are fun. Bury the TV
remote control.

If something is out of reach, it's a
challenge.

Furniture is to be slept on.

Practice whimpering pathetically.
There's no limit to what they'll do to
make you stop.

Be creative. There are over a hundred
uses for dirt.

Never let them sit for more than five minutes at the park. They took you there to play, didn't they?

Hide their copy of the dog-training manual.

Chairs are not just for sitting. They make dandy ramps for jumping.

If the vet promises you that it won't hurt, it's time to growl.

If someone you don't like tries to pick you up, make your whole body as stiff as a board.

When something has a hole, make it bigger.

If something fits inside your mouth, it could be food.

Bones taste better if you can take them away from another dog.

If you really work at it, you can pull down the drapes.

When they rake the leaves into a pile, put them back where they belong.

Bath time is only fun if they get wet, too.

If you barrel into the back of their knees, they'll fall down.

Practice splashing in puddles until you can get everyone around you wet.

With diligence, you can chew up a tennis shoe in less than an hour.

The microwave is your friend. Learn to identify the beeping sound it makes when food comes out.

Kibble is acceptable if there's no other food.

Check to make sure that Daddy's new watch is waterproof by dropping it into the toilet bowl.

Even though it smells like a tree, don't piddle on the table leg.

Squeaky toys are annoying. Chew out the squeaker.

Daddy's getting out of shape. Make *him* fetch the ball for *you*.

Your tail makes a great drumstick. Practice beating out rhythms on every handy surface.

Fertilizer makes the grass green. Why shouldn't it be good for the rug?

Never put your tail under Grandma's rocker.

Even if it smells like cowhide, looks like cowhide, and tastes like cowhide, you'll be in trouble if you chew the new couch.

A screen door never kept a determined dog inside.

A smart dog can always find a way to get back inside the house.

Teach them to shake paws with you. Then make them do it over and over and over.

You can drag all sorts of things in through the doggy door.

Mommy loves to buy new shoes. Hide one each, from several pairs.

If they leave without feeding you, don't panic. There's always a tasty morsel in the trash.

You're never too big to be a lapdog.

When the leash comes out, run around the room and let them chase you.

Choke collars do exactly that.

A closed door means there's something interesting going on inside.

If they let you out on a rainy day, immediately bark to come back in. You can do this over and over and over.

Always be the first one up the stairs.

Always be the first one down the stairs.

If you go in and out of the pickets on the fence, you can force them to drop the leash.

Always remember how to find your way home. It doesn't get any better than this.